best easy dayhikes

Sequoia and Kings Canyon National Parks

Laurel Scheidt

FALCON®

Guilford, Connecticut
An imprint of The Globe Pequot Press

AFALCONGUIDE®

Cover photo: Inga Spence/Index Stock
Maps: Blue Gecko Graphics

ISSN 1541-1397
ISBN 0-7627-1072-1

Manufactured in the United States of America
First Edition/Third Printing

Contents

Hikes in the Cedar Grove Area

Hikes in the Mineral King and South Fork Areas

Hikes in the Jennie Lakes Wilderness

Map Legend

US Highway	{00} {000}	Campground	▲	
State or Other Principal Road	(00) (000)	Picnic Area	⛉	
Forest Route	00 00000	Peak		9,782 ft.
Paved Road	▭▭▭▭▭▷	Information	❶	
Gravel Road	▭▭▭▷	Ranger Station/ Ranger Cabin	♠	
One Way Road	One Way	Cabin/Building	■	
Main Trail	●‒●‒‒●‒	Gate	•—•	
Secondary Trail	‒●‒‒‒‒●‒	Point of Interest	◘	
Trail Junction/ Entrance Station	□	View/Overlook	⪦	
Parking Area	Ⓟ	Pass/Saddle	) (	
River/Creek/Waterfall	～⫽	Tree/Grove	♠	
Bridge	‿‿	Fallen Tree/Log	✔	
Meadow/Marsh	⤓	National Forest/ Park Boundary		
Spring	⌀			
Dam	▬		N	
Prospect/Mine	✗	Map Orientation	↑	
Cave	⟋⊙⟍	Scale	0 0.5 1 Miles	

Overview Map

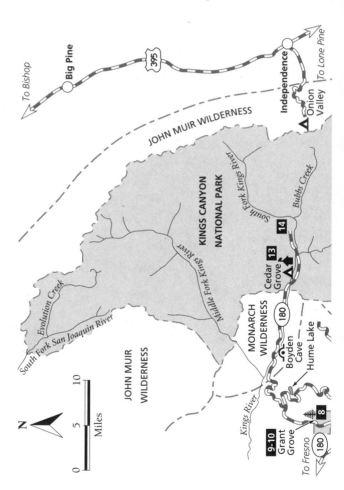

Sequoia and Kings Canyon National Parks

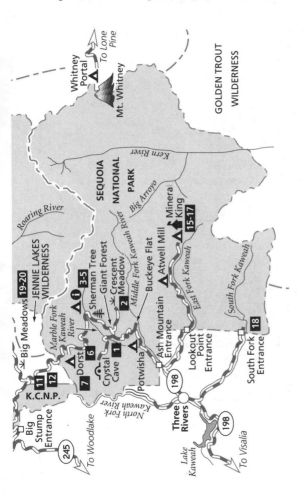

Ranking the Hikes

The following list ranks hikes in this guide from easiest to hardest.

Introduction

Sequoia and Kings Canyon have been called "hiker's parks" because most of their area is completely roadless. Trails abound for the day hiker as well as the backpacker.

Groves of giant sequoias, waterfalls, quiet streams and meadows, wilderness lakes, and mountaintop views are all within reach of the day hiker. While some trails get heavy use, on others you may not see a soul. Every trail in Sequoia and Kings Canyon will give you something special to remember, from tiny ladybugs to immense giant sequoias, which are some of the largest living things on earth.

The main hiking season in Sequoia and Kings Canyon is early summer through fall. Lower elevation hikes such as those in the foothills and South Fork areas are best in spring, when snow still obstructs trails at higher elevations. Trails tend to be more crowded on weekends and holidays and throughout the summer vacation period. The weather can turn at any time, so be prepared! A sunny day can turn into a cold and rainy one without much warning at higher elevations. Bears and mountain lions live in these parks and if you happen to see one, observe it from a safe distance. At lower elevations, watch out for rattlesnakes and ticks.

Visiting natural areas always imposes risks. You are responsible for your own safety. Take heed of posted warnings, be aware of your surroundings, and do not exceed your own limits. Also, leave your trip plans with a responsible party. Dial 911 for any medical emergency.

—*Laurel Scheidt*

Using This Guide

What Is a Best Easy Day Hike?

This hiking guide is an abridged version of *Hiking Sequoia and Kings Canyon National Parks*. The guide is designed to allow readers to choose hikes best suited to their abilities and time available. Most of the hikes are 1 to 6 miles in length and gain less than 2,000 feet in elevation. All of the hikes are on well marked trails that are easy to follow; most are suitable for novice hikers and families with children.

How This Guide Is Organized

I have grouped hikes together that begin in and travel through specific areas. These areas are arranged according to the popularity of the area and the area's accessibility.

Maps

Every day hiker should carry a trail map to avoid getting lost. The National Geographic/Trails Illustrated overview map of Sequoia and Kings Canyon (which has a few discrepancies) and inexpensive maps for Giant Forest, Lodgepole and Wolverton, Grant Grove, Cedar Grove, and Mineral King are available at the park visitor centers. Hikes not included on the maps mentioned above are usually covered on U.S. Geological Survey quad maps, which are also available at visitor centers.

The U.S. Forest Service topographic trail map for the Monarch and Jennie Lakes Wildernesses is available at local map and sporting goods stores and at Forest Service offices. For high-tech hikers with computers, the TOPO! Sequoia Kings Canyon and Surrounding Wilderness Areas CD-ROM covers the entire area; it is sold at map and sporting goods stores, and online at www.topo.com.

Types of Hikes

Different terms are used to describe the types of hikes included in this guide. These include:

- *Out-and-back:* Travel to a specific destination, then retrace your steps back to the trailhead.
- *Loop:* Start and finish at the same trailhead, with no (or very little) retracing of your steps.
- *Semi-loop:* Start and finish at the same trailhead, retracing a portion of your steps.

Elevation changes listed for each hike reflect only the overall change in elevation along a specific trail, and not ups and downs along the route.

Items Every Hiker Should Carry

- Two quarts of water per person
- Warm clothing and rain gear
- Hat with brim or sunglasses
- Food
- Map and compass
- Flashlight
- First-aid kit with bandages, moleskin, lip balm, insect repellent, and sunscreen
- Toilet paper and zip-locked bags for packing out used toilet paper

Zero Impact

Going into a wild area is like visiting a famous museum. You would not want to leave your mark on an art treasure in the museum. If everyone touring the museum left one little mark, the art would be quickly destroyed—and of what value is a big building full of trashed art? The same goes for pristine wildlands. If we all left a mark on the landscape, the backcountry would soon be spoiled.

A wilderness can accommodate human use as long as we tread it with care. But a few thoughtless or uninformed visitors can ruin a place for everyone who follows. All backcountry users have a responsibility to know and follow the rules of zero impact hiking.

Nowadays most wilderness users want to walk softly, but some aren't aware that the rules have changed. Often their actions are dictated by the outdated habits of a past generation of campers who cut green boughs for evening shelters, built campfires with fire rings, and dug trenches around tents. In the 1950s, these "camping rules" may have been acceptable. But such practices leave long-lasting scars, and today they are unacceptable. As the number of back-country visitors mushrooms, wild places are becoming rare, and many camping areas show unsightly signs of heavy use.

Consequently, a new code of ethics has developed to cope with the impact of the countless masses in search of a perfect backcountry experience. Today, we must leave no clue that we were there. Enjoy the wild, but strive for zero impact.

Three Falcon Zero-Impact Principles

- *Leave with everything you brought.*
- *Leave no sign of your visit.*
- *Leave the landscape as you found it.*

Most of us know better than to litter—in or out of the backcountry. Leave nothing, regardless of how small it is, along the trail or at a campsite. Pack out all trash, including orange peels, flip tops, cigarette butts, and gum wrappers. Also, pick up any trash that others have left behind.

Follow the established trail. Avoid cutting switchbacks and walking on vegetation beside the trail. Don't pick up "souvenirs," such as rock, antlers, or wildflowers. The next person wants to see them too, and collecting such souvenirs violates many regulations.

Avoid making loud noises on the trail or at trailheads. Be courteous—sound travels easily in the backcountry, especially across water.

If possible, use rest rooms or outhouses. Otherwise, carry a lightweight trowel to bury human waste 6 to 8 inches deep. Pack out used toilet paper. Keep human waste off the trail and at least 300 feet from any water source.

Finally, and perhaps most importantly, strictly follow the pack-in/pack-out rule. If you carry something into the backcountry, consume it or carry it out.

Follow these principles. Then put your ear to the ground and listen carefully. Thousands of people coming behind you are thanking you for your courtesy and good sense.

Upper Colony Mill Trail

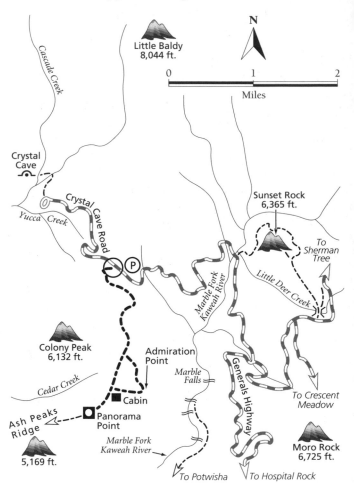

1
UPPER COLONY MILL TRAIL

Highlights: This trek follows the old dirt road that served as the entrance to Sequoia National Park and the Giant Forest before the Generals Highway opened in 1926.

Type of hike: Semi-loop.

Total distance: 5.2 or 5.8 miles.

Best months: May through June; October through early November.

Elevation change: 950 feet.

Maps: USGS Giant Forest, Sequoia National Park Giant Forest, or TOPO! Sequoia Kings Canyon CD-ROM.

Special considerations: The gate across Crystal Cave Road just west of the Marble Fork bridge is closed every night at 5 p.m. Be sure to leave the area before this time or you may get locked in.

Parking and trailhead facilities: There are no facilities at this trailhead. Rest rooms and water are available 2.3 miles farther west down the road at the Crystal Cave parking area when the cave is open for tours (from 11 A.M. to 4 P.M. between the months of May and September). The trail begins at the west end of the Colony Mill parking area, just past the large logs blocking the old dirt road.

Finding the trailhead: On the Generals Highway, drive 13.8 miles north from the Ash Mountain entrance station or 4.2 miles south from the General Sherman Tree area to

Crystal Cave Road. Turn onto the road and drive west for 4.1 miles, passing the Marble Fork bridge. The small Colony Mill parking area is located on the left (south) side of the road.

Key points:
0.0 Trailhead.
1.4 The trail forks.
2.4 Reach the old ranger station.
2.5 The trail forks again.
2.9 Take in the views at Panorama Point.
3.3 Return to the previous trail junction.
3.8 Rejoin the main trail.

The hike: The old park entrance road leads west, then curves south, dropping slightly through dogwoods and a shady mixed forest. Wild iris sometimes grows in the middle of the road. The wide path curves toward the southeast, climbing gently below Colony Peak. At the trail junction at 1.4 miles, keep left (southeast). The overgrown road to the right is your return route.

After crossing over a small ridge, the trail descends to Admiration Point. Beneath you is Marble Falls, though it may not be visible through the brush growing wildly on the hillside. In the east stand the peaks of the Great Western Divide, with Moro Rock in the foreground.

The trail curves west, through chamise, manzanita, and wildflowers in spring. At 2.4 miles you arrive at the old entrance station to Sequoia National Park. The dilapidated Colony Mill Ranger Station is obviously no longer in use. The road below this point was constructed mainly with hand tools by a utopian group known as the Kaweah Colonists. They erected an infamous portable sawmill nearby, in order to log the Giant Forest. In 1890 the establishment of Sequoia National Park thwarted the Colonists' plans. Thirteen years later the U.S. Cavalry extended the road (where you've been hiking) to the Giant Forest, making this the main route into the park until the Generals Highway opened in 1926.

The trail continues past toppled outhouses to the junction with your return route at 2.5 miles. Take the left (southwest) fork to Panorama Point, for more views to the east at 2.9 miles. Two abandoned trails lead off from this point: one to the highest point on Ash Peaks Ridge where a fire lookout was once located, the other downhill to the Generals Highway via Elk Creek. Both trails are now too overgrown for use. The Colony Mill Trail continues for another 7 miles west to North Fork Drive.

Retrace your steps to the junction with your return trail, now 3.3 miles into the hike. Keep left (north) at the fork and follow the overgrown route over the ridge. You may see mountain quail and their chicks in this lightly traveled area. At the junction with the main trail at 3.8 miles, turn left (north) and return to the parking area at 5.2 miles.

If you want to avoid any bushwhacking, turn around at Panorama Point and return the way you came, for a 5.8-mile round trip.

2
CRESCENT AND LOG MEADOWS

Highlights: This partially paved route takes you past one of John Muir's favorite meadows and to a real "log cabin." Wildlife frequents these meadows, and deer and bear sightings are common.

Type of hike: Loop.

Total distance: 1.7 miles.

Best months: June through October.

Elevation change: 340 feet.

Maps: USGS Giant Forest; Sequoia National Park Giant Forest; or TOPO! Sequoia Kings Canyon CD-ROM.

Parking and trailhead facilities: Rest rooms, water, and a picnic area are all available at this trailhead. The trail begins at the southeast end of the parking area, just south of the rest rooms.

Finding the trailhead: On the Generals Highway, drive 15.9 miles north from the Ash Mountain entrance station or 2.1 miles south from the General Sherman Tree area to Crescent Meadow Road. Turn right (east) and follow the narrow, winding road for 2.5 miles to its end at the Crescent Meadow parking area, passing the Moro Rock turnoff along the way.

Crescent and Log Meadows

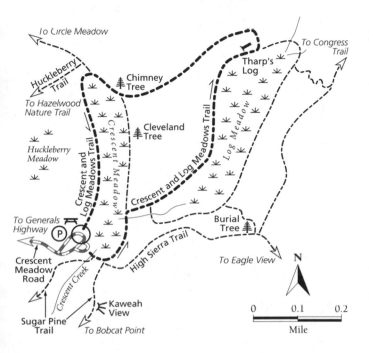

Key points:

0.0 Trailhead.

0.3 Pass the trail junction to the Cleveland Tree; stay right.

0.8 Arrive at Tharp's Log.

1.2 Reach Chimney Tree.

11

The hike: The paved path that begins this jaunt coincides with the start of the High Sierra Trail. After crossing Crescent Creek on two wooden footbridges you take the left (east) fork, leaving the celebrated trans-Sierra route, which continues to Eagle View and then heads into the backcountry. A large sign at the end of Crescent Meadow proclaims it the "Gem of the Sierra," a quote from John Muir. Wildflowers bloom amidst the green and yellow grasses. Shooting stars and leopard lilies appear in early season, lavender lupines in the middle of summer, and bright spears of meadow goldenrods near summer's end.

The trail travels north along the southeast rim of the meadow. At 0.3 mile, a dirt track leads left (north) to the Cleveland and Chimney Trees. Continue northeast on the paved path through the forest. Another dirt trail on the right loops around the east side of Log Meadow. The paved path takes you along the west side of Log Meadow, where, if the trail is not crowded, you may spot a bear or a doe with her young. Yellow-rumped and orange-crowned warblers often flit about in the trees above the trail.

The trail loses its pavement, and reaches Tharp's Log at 0.8 mile. Hale Tharp homesteaded the Log Meadow area long before the national park was established. He may have used this cabin—a fire-hollowed sequoia that was converted into a cabin—as a shelter while he grazed his cattle. A split-rail corral, overgrown with snowbrush, is barely visible behind a log bench.

From Tharp's Log, the unpaved footpath ascends the low ridge separating the two meadows, climbing over a large log with steps carved into it. The trail descends to the Chimney Tree and the junction with the Cleveland Tree trail, which heads south at 1.2 miles. Proceed west around the northern tip of Crescent Meadow before turning left (south). The path skirts the sunlit meadow before arriving back at the picnic area and the trailhead at 1.7 miles.

3
CONGRESS TRAIL

Highlights: This paved interpretive trail takes you to the General Sherman Tree, the largest living thing on earth, and to many other impressive "giants."
Type of hike: Loop.
Total distance: 1.9 miles.
Best months: June through October.
Elevation change: 705 feet.
Maps: USGS Giant Forest; Sequoia National Park Giant Forest; or TOPO! Sequoia Kings Canyon CD-ROM.
Parking and trailhead facilities: Rest rooms and water are available at the parking area. The trail begins at the General Sherman Tree, north of the parking area. Purchase an interpretive brochure near the General Sherman Tree or at a park visitor center.

Finding the trailhead: On the Generals Highway, drive 18.3 miles north from the Ash Mountain entrance station, or 2.2 miles south from Lodgepole, to the General Sherman Tree parking area. The parking area is on the east side of the Generals Highway. Overflow parking is available on the west side of the highway.

Congress Trail

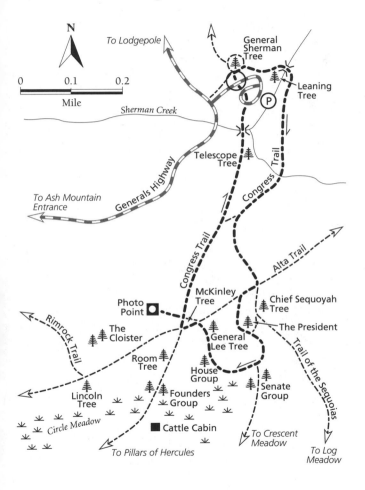

N

0   0.1   0.2
Mile

To Lodgepole

General Sherman Tree

Leaning Tree

Sherman Creek

P

Telescope Tree

Congress Trail

To Ash Mountain Entrance

Generals Highway

Congress Trail

Alta Trail

McKinley Tree

Photo Point

Chief Sequoyah Tree

The President

The Cloister

Rimrock Trail

General Lee Tree

Room Tree

House Group

Senate Group

Trail of the Sequoias

Lincoln Tree

Founders Group

Circle Meadow

Cattle Cabin

To Pillars of Hercules

To Crescent Meadow

To Log Meadow

Key points:
0.0 Trailhead.
0.6 Pass a cutoff trail.
0.9 Reach a four-way junction.
1.4 Reach another four-way junction.
1.7 Pass the cutoff trail.

The hike: Begin this journey at the General Sherman Tree. Named for William Tecumseh Sherman, a Union general in the Civil War, this giant sequoia is the largest living organism on earth. It is almost 275 feet tall and about 36.5 feet in diameter at its base, and weighs approximately 1,385 tons. After taking in this awesome sight, you will follow the paved path along the east side of the entrance road to the parking area. You will pass young sequoias on the way to the signed Congress Trail, named for some of the noteworthy trees along the trail.

A short downhill stretch brings you to a small bridge across Sherman Creek and to the Leaning Tree. The trail then begins a gradual climb. The route travels through the big trees, past many numbered stops described in the interpretive pamphlet. Pass the cutoff trail at 0.6 mile and continue to the four-way junction with the Trail of the Sequoias and the Alta Trail at 0.9 mile.

Follow the pavement to your right (west). You soon reach the fourth largest sequoia, known as the President. The Chief Sequoyah Tree is just up the side trail to the right (east) of the President; it is named in honor of the Cherokee Indian who developed a phonetic alphabet for his tribe.

16

The paved path goes on to a group of large sequoias dubbed The Senate. The footpath that leads through the center of these behemoths is the culmination of the Trail of the Sequoias. After passing a portion of Circle Meadow, the trail reaches a group of sequoias known as The House, named for the House of Representatives. After The House, you come upon the General Lee Tree. Another four-way junction is near the McKinley Tree at 1.4 miles. The trail to your left (south) leads to Circle Meadow; the Alta Trail ahead (west) leads to the site of the former Giant Forest Lodge, which has been removed to protect the giant sequoias. Turn right, heading north on the paved path.

On your left (west), a spur path leads to a photo point of the McKinley Tree, named for President William McKinley after his assassination in 1901. The trail descends, passing more interpretive stops as you approach the cutoff trail at 1.7 miles. Make your way through a tunnel in an enormous sequoia that fell across the trail in 1965. The pathway recrosses gurgling Sherman Creek on a footbridge and climbs back to the parking area at 1.9 miles.

Note: In late 2001, the National Park Service began work on improvements to the Congress Trail, repaving and making some minor route changes. The changes are intended to clean up trail junctions and make route-finding easier. Upon completion, there may be some slight variations to the hike described above.

Tokopah Falls

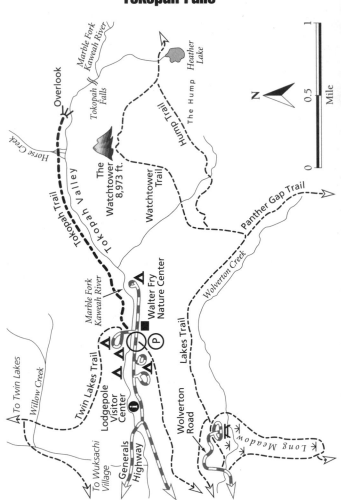

4
TOKOPAH FALLS

Highlights: This hike takes you to the head of glacially carved Tokopah Valley, which culminates at lovely Tokopah Falls.

Type of hike: Out-and-back.

Total distance: 3.8 miles.

Best months: June through October.

Elevation change: 635 feet.

Maps: USGS Triple Divide; Sequoia National Park Lodgepole and Wolverton; or TOPO! Sequoia Kings Canyon CD-ROM.

Parking and trailhead facilities: Rest rooms are available next to the Walter Fry Nature Center and at the Lodgepole Visitor Center. Water is available at the east end of the parking area and at the visitor center. The trail begins just east of the parking area, on the right side of the road, north of Log Bridge (which has been reconstructed, but has retained its original name).

Finding the trailhead: Take the Generals Highway south about 27 miles from the Big Stump entrance in Kings Canyon National Park, or north for a little more than 20 miles from the Ash Mountain entrance in Sequoia National Park, to Lodgepole. Take the road into Lodgepole, heading east past the visitor center to Lodgepole Campground. Tell the person at the gate you are going to the trailhead. Proceed to the parking area on the left (north) side of the road, before Log Bridge and across the road from the Walter Fry Nature Center.

Key points:
0.0 Trailhead.
1.4 Cross Horse Creek.
1.9 Reach the Tokopah Falls overlook.

The hike: The trail begins by following the north bank of the Marble Fork of the Kaweah River. A trailbed has been chiseled into a section of granite here. Be careful as you traverse the smooth, sometimes slippery rock.

As you enter the forest you may notice colorful tents and sounds of civilization in the campground across the river. Those reverberations soon fade away. Spur trails lead down to the river throughout this hike; be sure to keep to the left at these junctions, and keep to the right on the return trip. If you decide to explore these spur trails, exercise extreme caution near swift-moving areas of the river and during peak runoff periods in early summer.

Tokopah Valley was shaped by a glacier, much like Yosemite Valley and the Cedar Grove area of Kings Canyon. A view of the Watchtower, the large, pointed granite monolith on the south wall of the valley, opens up to your right (southeast). This crag was too solid to be ground down by the ice sheet; it seems to change shape as you travel on toward the falls. As you continue through firs and lodgepole pines, you pass small meadows where you may see a deer or bear.

The trail leads up and over a couple of small ledges before reaching the first branch of Horse Creek at 1.4 miles. Three footbridges help you cross the many-forked creek. The trail then cuts across a wash, which usually runs only in early spring and can be crossed on stones if water is present.

As you leave the forest, you gain a view of the falls in its entirety. The trail then winds through willows and boulders; it is edged with brilliant red penstemons in summer. As you near the falls overlook you may see marmots and even a pika among the talus blocks and boulders. The overlook is at 1.9 miles. A sign warns visitors not to continue up the canyon to the falls due to injuries and deaths that have occurred here in the past.

After enjoying a safe view of the falls, return the way you came (3.8 miles).

Heather Lake

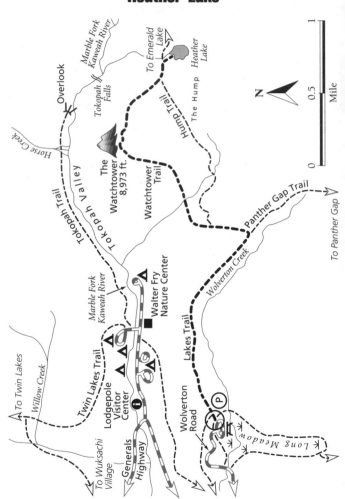

5
HEATHER LAKE

Highlights: This jaunt culminates at the first lake on the Lakes Trail. Heather Lake is a tranquil pool of water, its shores lined with red heather.

Type of hike: Out-and-back.

Total distance: 8.2 miles.

Best months: Mid-June through October.

Elevation change: 1,900 feet.

Maps: USGS Lodgepole; Sequoia National Park Lodgepole and Wolverton; or TOPO! Sequoia Kings Canyon CD-ROM.

Parking and trailhead facilities: Rest rooms and water are available at the south side of the parking area. The trail begins on the north side of the parking area.

Finding the trailhead: Drive 1.6 miles south from Lodgepole on the Generals Highway, or 0.5 mile north from the General Sherman Tree parking area, to signed Wolverton Road. Turn east and follow Wolverton Road for 1.5 miles to the parking area at its end.

Key points:
0.0 Trailhead.
0.1 Pass the spur trail to Lodgepole.
1.7 Meet the Panther Gap Trail junction.

2.0 Arrive at the Watchtower/Hump Trail junction.
4.1 Reach tranquil Heather Lake.

The hike: Begin by heading up some concrete steps and head north on the signed Lakes Trail. On your way uphill, you meet an unsigned trail to your left (west); this is part of the Long Meadow Trail. Continue around the curve to a junction at 0.1 mile with a connector trail leading to Lodgepole. Keep right (east). Almost immediately, you will pass another junction with the Long Meadow Trail.

Your path travels up a moraine deposited by the Tokopah glacier millions of years ago. The trail nears the tinkling sounds of Wolverton Creek and a lush meadow appears on the right (south).

The trail curves to the southeast, travels through clearings in the dense woodland, and crosses a creeklet. At the junction with the Panther Gap Trail at 1.7 miles, turn left (northeast). The path recrosses the same small watercourse and meets the Hump Trail at 2 miles. Keep left (northeast) on the Watchtower Trail, which is less steep and has better views from its cliffside route.

The trail climbs to a meadow, where you can cross its creek easily on stones. The grade steepens; you may see a marmot or hear one of their loud chirps as you climb. Moments later the trail switchbacks and deposits you next to the Watchtower, the colossal granite spire on the south side of Tokopah Valley.

After examining the Watchtower and Tokopah Falls 1,500 feet below, continue east on a shelf blasted out of the rock. Views up and down the valley seem endless. The trail is wide and easy to follow as it climbs, then descends to meet the other end of the Hump Trail. Enter a thinly forested area. At 4.1 miles, you reach Heather Lake, named for the red heather lining its shores. A short trail to the north leads to an open-air pit toilet (toilet paper is not supplied).

After taking in the peacefulness of Heather Lake, backtrack to the parking area at 8.2 miles.

6
LITTLE BALDY

Highlights: The summit of Little Baldy gives a spectacular view of the Silliman Crest, the Kaweah Peaks, and the lower portion of the Great Western Divide.

Type of hike: Out-and-back.

Total distance: 3.3 miles.

Best months: June through October.

Elevation change: 704 feet.

Maps: USGS Giant Forest; Sequoia National Park Lodgepole and Wolverton; or TOPO! Sequoia Kings Canyon CD-ROM.

Special considerations: During storms, there is a risk of being struck by lightning on the summit of Little Baldy. If you see dark clouds nearby, or observe hail, rain, thunder, or static electricity in the air, descend immediately.

Parking and trailhead facilities: No facilities are available at this trailhead. The trail begins on the east side of the road, marked by a large sign.

Finding the trailhead: Drive 6.6 miles north from Lodgepole on the Generals Highway, or 1.5 miles south from Dorst Campground, to the signed Little Baldy Saddle. Parking is available on both sides of the road.

Little Baldy

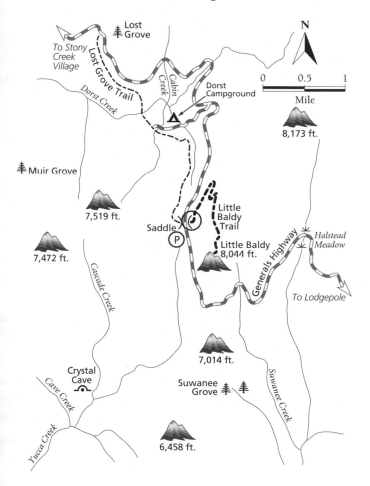

Key points:
0.0 Trailhead.
0.4 Enjoy the view of Big Baldy and Chimney Rock.
1.0 Enter a quiet wooded area.
1.3 Look out toward the Great Western Divide.
1.7 Attain the summit of Little Baldy.

The hike: The trail begins by climbing a few stone steps and a short switchback (not shown on some maps). At 0.1 mile, the end of this switchback, you may discern an old, abandoned trailbed that leads back to the road. Continue uphill on a long traverse through a thick forest of tall pine and fir trees. As you near the next switchback at 0.4 mile, a view opens up to the west, revealing Big Baldy and Chimney Rock. Many wildflowers grow here in summer. You may even see marmots among the large boulders above the path.

Continuing on this open, sometimes rocky portion of the trail, you meet two more switchbacks before the trail levels off. At 1 mile, a very quiet wooded area is a good place to stop and listen to the silence.

After leaving this peaceful place and rounding a hilltop at 1.3 miles, you begin to have views to the east of the Kaweahs and the Great Western Divide. The trail brings you through intermittent forest to the base of Little Baldy's granite dome, contours around the south side, and leads on to the summit at 1.7 miles.

Spanish Mountain and Obelisk are visible to the north. To the east are Mount Silliman, Alta Peak, the

Kaweah group, and the Great Western Divide extending south to Farewell Gap. In the foreground to the south-southeast, you can see the tip of Moro Rock and the Castle Rocks. On a clear day look west; you may even be able to see the San Joaquin Valley, a backdrop to Big Baldy Ridge and Chimney Rock.

After enjoying the view, retrace your steps to the trail-head (approximately 3.3 miles).

7
MUIR GROVE

Highlights: This hike takes you to a less frequently visited sequoia grove, with views of Big Baldy and Chimney Rock along the way.

Type of hike: Out-and-back.

Total distance: 4 miles.

Best months: June through October.

Elevation change: 848 feet.

Maps: USGS Muir Grove, or TOPO! Sequoia Kings Canyon CD-ROM.

Parking and trailhead facilities: Rest rooms and water are available across the road from the trailhead. The signed trail begins on the west side of the road between the group campground entrance and the amphitheater parking area.

Finding the trailhead: Follow the Generals Highway 5 miles south of Stony Creek Village or 8.2 miles north of Lodgepole to the Dorst Campground entrance. Drive west into the campground. Follow the signs to the amphitheater and a parking area at 0.9 mile, just beyond the group campground entrance.

Key points:
0.0 Trailhead.
0.1 The trail forks.
0.6 Cross the first creek.

Muir Grove

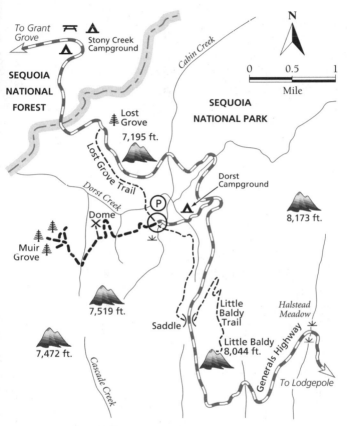

1.0 Reach a side trail to the dome overlook.
1.6 Cross the second creek.
2.0 Enter Muir Grove.

The hike: The trail begins by dipping to cross a tributary of Dorst Creek on a wooden footbridge. The trail then rises to pass above the group campground. Descend a switchback, and meet a north-trending trail to Dorst Creek at 0.1 mile. Follow the fork to the left (west), the signed Muir Trail; a fern-filled meadow is on your right. The trail travels through a thick fir forest, where you may hear the peaceful song of the hermit thrush.

Pass over granite slabs, and step across another tributary at 0.6 mile, before coming to a fork. What appears to be a climber's trail departs from the base of a couple of long switchbacks; this side trail continues straight toward the base of the granite dome above, and is feebly blocked by some branches. Turn left (south), traveling uphill. At 1 mile, you arrive at a path leading to the high point of this dome, with a view of Big Baldy and the east face of Chimney Rock. You can also see the sequoias of Muir Grove, this hike's destination, on the ridge west of here.

The trail passes into the trees again, then enters a rocky area, traversing a steep portion of loose rock. Watch your step. After reentering the forest, the trail comes to another tributary at 1.6 miles. Those with good balance can cross on a large fallen tree. If you prefer a lower crossing, you will find some stones to aid your passage a few steps past the tree. Now the path narrows and becomes slightly overgrown, but remains easy to follow. Continue up the steep hillside until you reach a gigantic sequoia at the entrance to Muir Grove at 2 miles.

There is a myriad of paths to explore. A short track to the left ends abruptly in a group of giant sequoias. The path to your right travels uphill, splits, rejoins, and leads to a sequoia hollowed out by fire; it ends at a lupine-covered hillside. Another footpath proceeds straight ahead into a group of sequoias, fizzling out just past them. And finally, the route heading downhill to the southwest is the last remnant of the main trail. The path used to continue to Skagway Grove, Hidden Spring, and Crystal Cave. That section of the trail has not been maintained in more than 20 years. The route now ends about 50 feet from an immense sequoia that fell across the trail, guaranteeing its return to a natural state.

After you have explored the grove, return the way you came (4 miles).

8
BIG STUMP LOOP

Highlights: This interpretive trail takes you through an area that was heavily logged in the 1880s. The stumps and fallen trees now serve as a reminder of how important it is to protect our environment. Although General Grant National Park was established in 1890 and incorporated in Kings Canyon National Park in 1940, Big Stump Basin was not included until 1965.

Type of hike: Loop.

Total distance: 2 miles.

Best months: May through October.

Elevation change: 540 feet.

Maps: USGS General Grant Grove; Kings Canyon National Park Grant Grove; or TOPO! Sequoia Kings Canyon CD-ROM.

Parking and trailhead facilities: Rest rooms, water, picnic tables, and barbecues are available at the parking area. The trail begins on the south side of the parking area, near the rest rooms. You may purchase an interpretive booklet for this trail from a coin-operated machine at the trailhead and also at the park visitor center.

Finding the trailhead: From the Big Stump entrance station on California Highway 180, drive 0.6 mile to the Big Stump parking area, which is on the left (west) side of the road.

Big Stump Loop

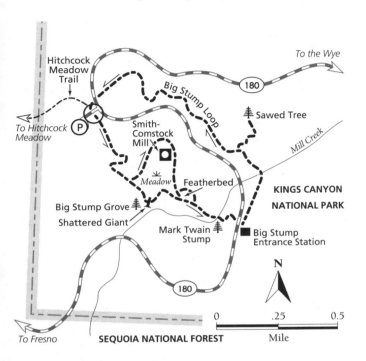

Key points:

0.0 Trailhead.

0.3 Reach the first trail fork.

0.6 Reach the second trail fork.

1.0 The trail crosses CA 180.

1.3 A side trail leads to the Sawed Tree.

The hike: As you head downhill (southeast), you almost immediately come to the Resurrection Tree. This giant's top was destroyed by lightning, and it is now "resurrecting" a new one. Beyond lies the Shake Pile, a toppled sequoia that was chiseled apart to make fence posts, roof shingles, and grape stakes. Though extremely rot and fire resistant, sequoia wood is very brittle; because of the immense size of these trees, they often shattered when they were felled.

At 0.3 mile the trail forks. Take the route to the left (east). It leads to the Burnt Monarch, known to the loggers as Old Adam. This huge, burned-out sequoia was used to store snow, allowing for ice in the summer months when the logging mill was in operation.

The trail continues to two sequoias planted in 1888. They have reached great heights in their hundred years, but not the girths of the old "giants." An abandoned road grade joins the trail just beyond these trees. Farther down the trail, a meadow serves as the site of the Smith-Comstock Mill. All that remains are the wood posts of the foundation sticking up through the grass to your right (west). Notice the piles of reddish brown sawdust that still remain more than one hundred years later.

A bit farther down the path is a side trail to the Featherbed. This trench was dug and lined with branches from other felled trees to cushion the fall of one of the "Big Trees." Observant hikers may spot other featherbeds in the area. At 0.6 mile the trail forks again. Turn right (west), traveling around the little meadow to the Shattered Giant. This tree smashed into so many pieces that it was practically unsalvageable. Now it serves as a bridge over the tiny tributary that flows through the meadow.

Retrace your steps around the meadow to the previous junction and turn right (east). Pass another portion of the Featherbed loop and cross Mill Creek on a wooden bridge. On the other side is the Mark Twain Stump. This sequoia was felled in 1891 so the American Museum of Natural History in New York could exhibit a slice. Steps lead to the top of the stump, and standing in the center gives you an even better idea of how large these trees really are. Also visible are the healed burn scars from fires the tree survived.

From the Mark Twain Stump the trail makes a short climb to CA 180 at 1 mile. Follow the crosswalk and continue uphill on the other side. Traveling through the forest, you reach the side trail to the Sawed Tree at 1.3 miles. Turn right (northeast) and take the path up a few short switchbacks to this survivor. When loggers realized the tree could not be felled in the direction they wanted, they moved on. The Sawed Tree still continues to heal.

To return to the main trail, retrace your steps. At the last switchback, an abandoned section of trail to the left (south) is passable until just before it reaches the main trail, where it is blocked by thorny ceanothus or snowbrush. If you venture off here, return to the main trail; stay right (northwest) and pass through more forest and manzanita clearings to a short downhill. The path then follows a long, thin meadow to a large culvert that allows you to pass under CA 180 and meet the start of the Hitchcock Meadow Trail. Turn left (south) and climb to the parking area (2 miles).

9
GENERAL GRANT LOOP

Highlights: This paved interpretive trail takes you through the heart of the General Grant Grove to the General Grant Tree. Named for Ulysses S. Grant, this tree has been declared the nation's Christmas Tree and a living National Shrine honoring Americans who died in war. The trail also passes the historic Gamlin Cabin.

Type of hike: Loop.
Total distance: 0.8 mile.
Best months: May through October.
Elevation change: 220 feet.
Maps: USGS General Grant Grove; Kings Canyon National Park Grant Grove; or TOPO! Sequoia Kings Canyon CD-ROM.
Parking and trailhead facilities: Rest rooms and water are available at this large parking area. The paved trail begins at the large sign on the north side of the parking area. You may purchase an interpretive pamphlet for this trail from the coin-operated machine at the trailhead or at the Grant Grove Visitor Center.

Finding the trailhead: From the Big Stump entrance station, drive north on California Highway 180, past Grant Grove Village, to the junction with the road leading to the Grant Tree. Turn left (west) and drive to the Grant Tree parking area, which is 4.1 miles from the entrance station.

General Grant Loop

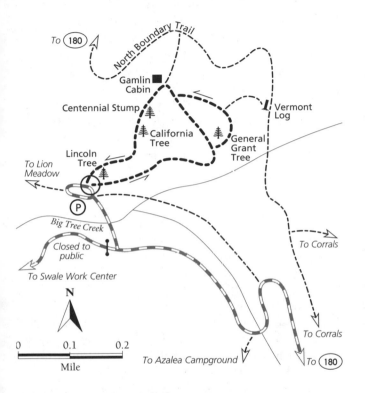

The hike: Begin this paved loop by taking the right fork to the Robert E. Lee Tree, the 13th largest tree in the world. Many sequoia groves were explored around the time of the Civil War, and some of the trees were given names of those made famous by that conflict. The General Grant

Tree is farther along the route. First, proceed just past the east end of the tree known as the Fallen Monarch to Photo Point. From this alcove you can take a picture of the entire Grant Tree from base to crown. Continuing on, you reach young sequoias that were planted around 1949. The trees contrast in size because of the different amounts of water and light each receives.

While giant sequoias are the main attraction, they are not the only trees in the grove. A sign describes the other trees, including white fir, incense cedar, sugar pine, and ponderosa pine. The Tennessee Tree, a giant sequoia, and Pacific dogwood trees are just ahead. If you are here in June, the dogwoods may be covered with soft, white blossoms.

Next you arrive at this trail's namesake, the General Grant Tree. This tree is the world's third largest living organism. It has a greater base diameter than any other sequoia. An unpaved trail circles the General Grant Tree, and meets a side trail that leads you to the Vermont Log (which fell in 1985).

On the main trail, continue on to the Gamlin Cabin. Built by the Gamlin brothers in 1872, this historic cabin served as the first ranger station for General Grant National Park, which was included in Kings Canyon National Park in 1940. Parts of the cabin have been restored, and a concrete foundation has been added to preserve the structure.

If you wish to visit North Grant View, another good photo opportunity, take the trail to the right (east) of Gamlin Cabin and proceed a few hundred feet uphill to the North Boundary Trail. Turn left (west) at the junction, walk in a short distance, and look back (southeast) toward the Grant Tree. The top-to-bottom view provides a different perspective from that at Photo Point.

Beyond the Gamlin Cabin you will find the Fire-Damaged Trees, which illustrate the fire resistance of sequoias, and the Centennial Stump. This stump is all that remains of a sequoia felled in 1875 so that a 16-foot section could be taken to the Centennial Exhibition in Philadelphia the following year. The tree was cut into segments for transportation and reassembled at the exhibition. Spectators thought it was many trees put together to resemble a single big tree, and dubbed it the "California Hoax." Later the stump was known as the "School Stump," as Sunday School classes were held on it during the logging era.

The route continues to the California Tree, which was struck by lightning in 1967. A park forester climbed this tree with a fire hose and put out the blaze to preserve the sequoia grove. The Oregon Tree View is just down the trail and to the right (northwest). The route has now looped to the west end of the Fallen Monarch. This huge tree sheltered the Gamlin brothers and others; it has been used as a hotel and saloon; and the U.S Cavalry, stabled their horses here while patrolling General Grant National Park.

As you near the end of the loop you reach the Lincoln Tree and a view of the Twin Sisters, two sequoias that have fused together on the west side of the parking area. When you have reached the parking area, you will notice the group of mature sequoias to your left, known as the Happy Family. These trees are about the same age and probably sprouted after a very intense fire cleared the spot where they have grown. The loop ends at 0.8 mile.

North Grove and Dead Giant Loops

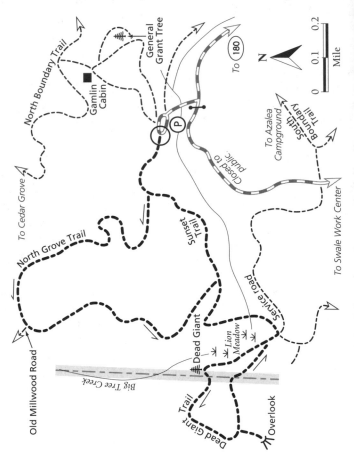

10
NORTH GROVE AND DEAD GIANT LOOPS

Highlights: This hike takes you through the northern portion of the General Grant Grove, past an old logging camp road and to the overlook of a beautiful lake.

Type of hike: Loop.

Total distance: 2.5 miles.

Best months: May through October.

Elevation change: 775 feet.

Maps: USGS Hume and USGS General Grant Grove; Kings Canyon National Park Grant Grove; or TOPO! Sequoia Kings Canyon CD-ROM.

Parking and trailhead facilities: Rest rooms and water are available at this large parking area. The trail begins at the westernmost lower parking area (reserved for RVs and trailers) at the gate signed "North Grove Loop."

Finding the trailhead: From the Big Stump entrance station, drive north on California Highway 180, past Grant Grove Village, to the junction with the road leading to the Grant Tree. Turn left (west) and drive to the Grant Tree parking area, which is 4.1 miles from the entrance station.

Key points:
0.0 Trailhead.
0.1 Reach the North Grove Trail junction.

0.6 Pass the Old Millwood Road junction.
1.1 Meet the first Sunset Trail junction.
1.3 Meet the Dead Giant Trail junction.
1.7 Arrive at the Sequoia Lake overlook.
1.9 Reach the second Sunset Trail junction.

The hike: The trail begins by following a closed road, which is also part of the Sunset Trail. Hike downhill through the dappled light of the shady forest. At 0.1 mile you reach the North Grove Trail junction. Turn right (northwest) on the North Grove Trail. The wide path winds between numerous sequoias while continuing to descend. At 0.6 mile you arrive at the unsigned junction with the Old Millwood Road, which resembles a small gully leading into the brush to your right (northwest). If you step through the overgrowth, you will see the gully widen to a one-lane dirt road. The Old Millwood Road leads 2.3 miles (with an elevation loss of 920 feet) to the site of Millwood, an old logging camp.

Beyond the junction, the trail climbs past an immense burned sequoia, and more of the "giants" before returning to the closed road. At 1.1 miles, you will reach the junction with the Sunset Trail. Turn right (south) and follow the road around pretty Lion Meadow. At 1.3 miles, you reach the junction with the Dead Giant Trail. Turn right (northwest) on the first and lower of two parallel paths. (You will return via the other trail.) The path travels above the edge of the deep green meadow and brings you to the Dead Giant, a large, girdled sequoia that still stands.

The trail turns to the southwest and climbs uphill past a trail sign, to the top of the ridge, through clearings in the manzanita. As the wide track levels, another trail sign indicates a left turn. Continue straight ahead to the Sequoia Lake overlook at 1.7 miles. Framed by cedars and pines, this sapphire blue lake is manmade. The Sanger Lumber Company dammed Sequoia Creek in 1889 to supply water for the flume that supported logging operations in the area. The flume stretched 54 miles to the town of Sanger and cost $300,000 to construct.

After viewing the lake, return to the previous trail sign and turn right (east). Follow the trail downhill, back into the forest. At 1.9 miles, you meet the closed road. Turn left (north) onto the road, following it past the two junctions with the North Grove Trail and back to the trailhead at 2.5 miles.

Hart Tree Loop

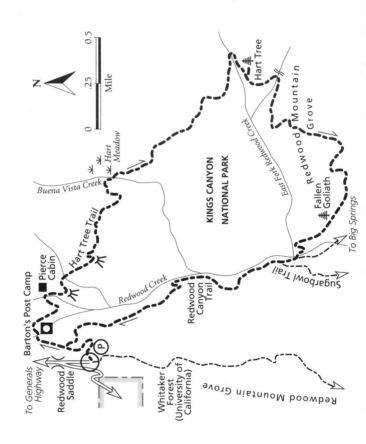

11
HART TREE LOOP

Highlights: This jaunt takes you to an old logging camp, a sequoia "log cabin," a pretty meadow, and a waterfall, all while traveling through the largest sequoia grove left standing on the planet.

Type of hike: Loop.

Total distance: 7.2 miles.

Best months: May through June; October through November.

Elevation change: 1,300 feet.

Maps: USGS General Grant Grove, or TOPO! Sequoia Kings Canyon CD-ROM.

Parking and trailhead facilities: A new outhouse is located at this trailhead but no water is available. The trail begins at the southwest end of the parking area, to the left of the bulletin board, and is signed "Hart Tree" and "Redwood Canyon."

Finding the trailhead: From the Big Stump entrance, drive south on the Generals Highway for 5.3 miles to Quail Flat. Turn right (south) onto the dirt road across from the paved road leading to Hume Lake. Drive approximately 7 miles to a junction at a large, modern cabin. Take the left (southeast) fork, which leads through a fallen sequoia and continues for another 0.2 mile to the parking area.

Key points:

0.0 Trailhead.
0.3 Meet the Redwood Canyon Trail junction.
0.5 Reach the Barton's Post Camp.
0.8 Reach the Pierce Cabin.
1.7 Reach a viewpoint.
1.9 Cross Buena Vista Creek.
3.0 Cross the East Fork of Redwood Creek.
3.5 Cross a creek near a waterfall.
4.7 Admire the Fallen Goliath.
5.2 Cross Redwood Creek.
5.3 Pass the Sugarbowl Trail.
6.9 Meet the Hart Tree Trail junction.

The hike: The wide trail (once a dirt road) heads south (downhill), past a fire hydrant and through mixed firs, pines, and giant sequoias. A view of Buena Vista Peak appears as the path rounds a turn and switchbacks. The junction with the Redwood Canyon trail is at 0.3 mile. Turn left (north) onto the Hart Tree Trail; the other path will be your return route.

Wild strawberries carpet the forest floor as you proceed. After stepping across fledgling Redwood Creek, you arrive at Barton's Post Camp at 0.5 mile. Large sequoia stumps and a few felled trees are the only evidence of the small-scale logging operation that manufactured fence posts here in the late 1800s.

The path crosses a small ridge and dips across an unnamed brook before reaching the deteriorating Pierce

Cabin at 0.8 mile. This fire-hollowed sequoia had shingles, fireplaces, and a door added to make it habitable at one time; today it is sadly collapsing. Climb onto to a granite-and-manzanita-covered knob at 0.9 mile. There, a few steps off the trail will give you an excellent view of the crowns of sequoias growing on Redwood Mountain, to the west.

After the viewpoint, you descend to cross another unnamed creeklet at 1 mile. The trail rises again, ascending a switchback, then traveling through oaks. Beyond another easily spanned rivulet, climb to a rocky knoll at 1.7 miles. Look west for views of Redwood Mountain and south toward Big Baldy Ridge (Hike 12), and the Redwood Canyon.

The trail then drops down through wild roses to lovely Hart Meadow, with Buena Vista Peak as the backdrop. At 1.9 miles you advance gingerly through a muddy area at the lower end of the meadow. Here, the trail crosses a couple of branches of Buena Vista Creek, which is lined with white mountain violets and sword ferns.

The route mounts the next ridge, then passes through the entire length of a fire-hollowed sequoia. (A bypass is available for the claustrophobic.) You wind your way down through fallen "giants" to the East Fork of Redwood Creek at 3 miles. This creek crossing can be a little tricky in early season if you are not wearing waterproof boots.

The trail ascends to a steep spur path at 3.2 miles, flanked by two signs and leading to the Hart Tree. At one time this behemoth was ranked as the fourth largest sequoia in the world, but other trees have surpassed it. The route then descends to a pretty, unnamed creek with a peaceful waterfall and an easy crossing on stones at 3.5 miles. A muddy seep intersects the path on the other side of this creek.

Begin the long decline to the bottom of the canyon, crossing one more tiny brook at 3.9 miles. Along the way you may spot tiny winter wrens darting around the many sequoia trunks near grassy areas.

After passing through large zones of wild rose and bear clover, you reach the immense Fallen Goliath at 4.7 miles. The path descends to Redwood Creek and a campsite to the right (north) at 5.2 miles. This crossing can be tricky without waterproof boots in early season, but the creek is easily crossed on stones in the fall. Alders and dogwoods line the creek, the latter decorated with delicate white blooms in June. Autumn brings an exhilarating color show, as the deciduous trees turn beautiful hues of light green, gold, and red.

On the other side of the creek you come to a junction with the Redwood Canyon Trail; turn right (northwest). At 5.3 miles you pass the junction with the Sugarbowl Trail as your path climbs gradually along meandering Redwood Creek. The route switchbacks as it moves up the slope from the watercourse, continuing past many "Big Trees" and working its way around three sequoias that have fallen across the old roadbed. At 6.9 miles, you reach the junction with the Hart Tree Trail. Turn left and retrace your steps to the parking area at 7.2 miles.

12
BIG BALDY RIDGE

Highlights: This trip takes you to a striking 360-degree view of Kings Canyon and Sequoia National Parks from the summit of Big Baldy. It continues on to a less visited view of the west face of Chimney Rock.
Type of hike: Out-and-back.
Total distance: 5.6 miles.
Best months: June through October.
Elevation change: 1,275 feet.
Maps: USGS General Grant Grove, or TOPO! Sequoia Kings Canyon CD-ROM.
Special considerations: During a storm, there is a risk of being struck by lightning on the summit of Big Baldy. If you see dark clouds nearby, or observe hail, rain, thunder, or static electricity in the air, descend immediately. There are also steep drop-offs around the summit; exercise caution.
Parking and trailhead facilities: There are no facilities at this trailhead. The closest facilities are at Stony Creek Village, 4.8 miles south on the Generals Highway. The trailhead begins on the southwest side of the parking area.

Finding the trailhead: From the Big Stump entrance, drive south on the Generals Highway for 8.4 miles, or north 4.8 miles from Stony Creek Village, to the signed parking turnout on the southwest side of a large, blind curve just west of Big Meadows Road. If the parking area is full,

Big Baldy Ridge

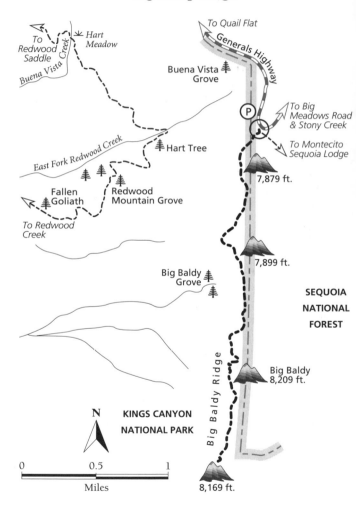

To Quail Flat

Generals Highway

Hart Meadow

To Redwood Saddle

Buena Vista Creek

Buena Vista Grove

P

To Big Meadows Road & Stony Creek

To Montecito Sequoia Lodge

Hart Tree

East Fork Redwood Creek

7,879 ft.

Fallen Goliath

Redwood Mountain Grove

7,899 ft.

To Redwood Creek

SEQUOIA

NATIONAL

FOREST

Big Baldy Grove

Big Baldy Ridge

Big Baldy
8,209 ft.

N

KINGS CANYON

NATIONAL PARK

0   0.5   1

Miles

8,169 ft.

another large turnout is available on the south side of the road, a little farther to the east on the Generals Highway.

Key points:
0.0 Trailhead.
2.1 Arrive at Big Baldy Summit.
2.8 Reach a high point with a view of Chimney Rock.

The hike: The trail enters the forest and meets a trail from the Montecito Sequoia Lodge. The Montecito trail is on private property; unless you are a guest at the lodge, do not enter the area. The Big Baldy Ridge trail winds between large boulders, chinquapin, and snowbrush beneath tall firs and pines. Ascend through an open, rocky area edged with manzanita, then go back into the woods. The route dips slightly and climbs again, passing many colorful wildflowers, notably skyrockets and penstemons in summer.

Entering another granitic area, you round a small dome and proceed up the ridge. As the trail levels a bit, a view of the summit opens up to the south. You reenter the trees and rise again, soon reaching a penstemon-lined switchback. The trail contours around the east side of the high point, just below the ridgecrest. As the trail swings up toward the summit, you pass a notch in the ridge that gives you a glimpse of the extreme drop-off.

At 2.1 miles you reach the summit of Big Baldy at 8,209 feet. The views are spectacular. To the north are Nelson Mountain and Eagle Peak near Courtright Reservoir, Spanish Mountain, Obelisk, Castle Peak, Mount Goddard, and jagged peaks in northern Kings

Canyon National Park. Nearest to you, in the north, is Buena Vista Peak. To the east the Great Western Divide and the Kaweah Peaks serve as a backdrop for Mount Silliman and Alta Peak. To the southeast are the peaks surrounding Mineral King, including Sawtooth Peak. To the west, Redwood Canyon, Redwood Mountain, and the smog-shrouded San Joaquin Valley are visible.

Leaving the summit, the trail continues south, along the west side of the short, stout summit pinnacles. It leads down, around the east side of the next dome, through rocky terrain. You descend to a saddle with a view of a pond and a meadow in the Pierce Valley to the west, and of the Sunrise Bowl just below you to the east. A metal-roofed structure and radio tower are found here. The path rounds another dome and travels through open forest to reach a portion of trail completely covered by crushed rock. A tree has fallen across the trail here; you may have to make your way over the obstacle if it has not been cleared away.

Your path then enters a forested area with many birds, including nuthatches, western bluebirds, and western tanagers. As you climb out of the forest, watch for a nice view of Chimney Rock and Little Baldy through the trees. The trail ascends, winding through talus blocks on the west side of a lower outcrop of Big Baldy Ridge at 2.8 miles. At an elevation of 8,169 feet, the views to the east of Chimney Rock and Little Baldy are exceptional; the Great Western Divide looms in the background. To the west are lower Redwood Canyon, Eshom Valley, and the San Joaquin Valley. Enjoy the views before backtracking to the parking area at 5.6 miles.

13
ROARING RIVER FALLS TO ZUMWALT MEADOW

Highlights: From billowing Roaring River Falls to peaceful Zumwalt Meadow, this hike is ideal for a picnic lunch or just relaxing.

Type of hike: Semi-loop.

Total distance: 3.9 miles.

Best months: Late May through October.

Elevation change: Minimal.

Maps: USGS The Sphinx; Kings Canyon National Park Cedar Grove; or TOPO! Sequoia Kings Canyon CD-ROM.

Parking and trailhead facilities: There are no facilities at this trailhead. Parking is available on the south side of California Highway 180, on either side of the bridge spanning the Roaring River. An interpretive pamphlet for the Zumwalt Meadow Trail can be purchased at its parking area and at park visitor centers. The trail begins on the south side of the parking area, east of the bridge.

Finding the trailhead: On CA 180, drive approximately 32 miles north, then east, of Grant Grove, past Cedar Grove, to the Roaring River Falls parking area on the right (south).

Roaring River Falls to Zumwalt Meadow

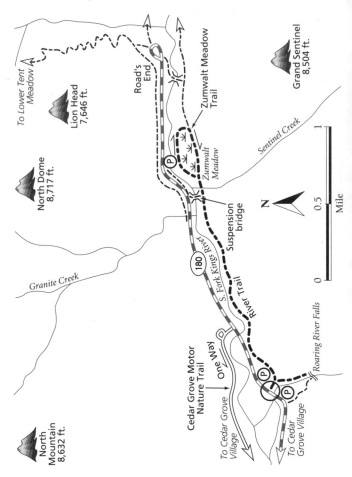

Key points:

0.0 Trailhead.

0.1 Check out Roaring River Falls.

0.2 Return to the River Trail junction.

1.6 Pass the suspension bridge.

1.7 Meet the Zumwalt Meadow Trail.

2.3 Arrive at the River Trail junction.

2.5 Pass the Zumwalt Meadow Trail junction.

3.8 Return to the Roaring River Trail junction.

The hike: The paved trail begins by following the Roaring River. In a few hundred feet you reach the River Trail, your route to Zumwalt Meadow. For now, continue straight ahead (south) to the falls at 0.1 mile.

As you approach the overlook, you will hear the roar of rushing water plunging into the blue-green pool that fills this granite bowl. Shrubs and small trees cling to the cliffs, which seem to reach straight up to the sky. When the falls are at their peak, mist douses those standing at the over-look. Only the lower portion of Roaring River Falls is vis-ible; the upper cascades are inaccessible. (Do not venture up the canyon on side trails. Others have been injured or killed trying to do so.)

After enjoying the falls safely, backtrack to the River Trail junction at 0.2 mile and make a right (east) turn. The rocky, open trail travels close to the road at first, but soon enters a shady forest along the South Fork of the Kings River. Continue on through the forest and clearings laced with the scent of incense cedar. After climbing a couple of rocky knolls, you come to the suspension bridge that leads to the Zumwalt Meadow Trail parking area, where an interpretive pamphlet can be purchased, at 1.6 miles.

Continue straight (east), and cross the usually dry Sentinel Creek—be prepared to rock hop if the creek is flowing. Meet the Zumwalt Meadow Trail junction at 1.7 miles. Turn left (northeast) and cross a seasonal creek on a small footbridge. North Dome and Lion Head rise above the trees to the north, while the Grand Sentinel towers above the meadow to the south. The trail travels along a boardwalk through the fragile meadow, then enters a shady forest while following the Kings River. Pause to enjoy the many tree-framed views of the meadow, accompanied by the peaceful splashing and rippling of the river. You may see a hummingbird, a dipper, or even a deer if the trail is not crowded.

Two spur trails on your left (east) connect with the River Trail as the path begins to leave the forest. After passing between two large boulders, the route reaches the main junction with the River Trail at 2.3 miles. Turn right (west) and begin a short climb. With Zumwalt Meadow visible below, the trail winds through a moonscape of talus blocks at the base of the Grand Sentinel. The trail dips, rises again, and recrosses the seasonal creek.

At 2.5 miles you reach the Zumwalt Meadow Trail junction and complete the loop portion of the trip. Retrace your steps on the remainder of your journey, returning to Roaring River parking area at 3.9 miles.

14
MIST FALLS

Highlights: This outing takes you to delightful Mist Falls.
Type of hike: Out-and-back.
Total distance: 8.2 miles.
Best months: Mid-June through October.
Elevation change: 528 feet.
Maps: USGS The Sphinx; Kings Canyon National Park Cedar Grove; or TOPO! Sequoia Kings Canyon CD-ROM.
Special considerations: This trail can be very hot; be sure to get an early start. Also, the trail is used by horseback riders. Please remember proper trail etiquette by stepping off the trail on the downhill side and waiting quietly until the horses have passed. Stay in plain view of the horses; they may think you are a wild animal and bolt if you are hidden behind a rock or tree. Finally, mountain lions frequent this area. You are advised not to hike solo.
Parking and trailhead facilities: Rest rooms, a water spigot, and an information center are located at the east end of the day-use parking area. The trail begins near the information center.

Finding the trailhead: Follow California Highway 180 north, then east, for approximately 30 miles from Grant Grove to Cedar Grove. The trailhead is approximately 5.6 miles past Cedar Grove Village at the Road's End parking area.

Mist Falls

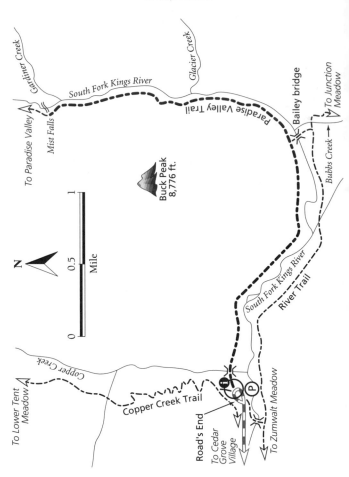

Key points:
0.0 Trailhead.
2.1 The trail forks.
4.1 Arrive at Mist Falls.

The hike: The trail starts at the information center and travels through sunny woods. Cross the Copper Creek bridge; the bridge is north of the Kanawyer's Store site, which served cattlemen and sheepherders heading into the backcountry in the early days. John Muir had even visited the old supply point, but it was torn down in the late 1920s. The Cedar Grove Ranger Station displays a picture of the store during its heyday.

Several side trails lead down to the river on the right (south), while the Grand Sentinel towers above on the south side of the canyon. Large gray squirrels scamper about, especially in the fall, when they are gathering acorns and pine cones for the winter. The path advances through manzanita clearings in the pockets of forest, then crosses a rocky knoll. Enter a shady area thick with green horsetails and reach a trail junction at 2.1 miles. To the right (south), the Bubbs Creek Trail leads across a Bailey bridge. Continue straight ahead (northeast) and uphill.

Soon you gain a view of the confluence of Bubbs Creek. The path dips and rises through the shade of cedars, oaks, and firs, with an understory of ferns and horsetails as it passes below Buck Peak. When you have climbed and switchbacked through mixed forest, a view of The Sphinx opens up down the canyon behind you. The path ascends a bit more with views of lacy cascades on the river below, before reaching the deluge of Mist Falls at 4.1 miles. In early season a cool mist wafts through the air, making this a wonderfully refreshing rest stop.

Watch your step in this area, as the rocks near the falls are slippery and dangerous. After you have enjoyed your destination, retrace your steps to the parking area at 8.2 miles.

15
COLD SPRINGS NATURE TRAIL

Highlights: This easy ramble takes you through meadows and aspen groves along the East Fork of the Kaweah River, giving you nice views of the surrounding peaks. It also leads to the former site of the mining settlement of Beulah.

Type of hike: Semi-loop.

Total distance: 2 miles.

Best months: June through October.

Elevation change: 340 feet.

Maps: Sequoia National Park Mineral King (the trail is not shown on other maps).

Parking and trailhead facilities: Rest rooms are located at the picnic area, and water is available in the Cold Springs Campground. If you park at the picnic area, follow the road west to the Cold Springs Campground entrance and a small parking turnout. Turn left (south). Cross the bridge and turn left again, now heading east. The signed nature trail begins next to campsite 6.

Finding the trailhead: From central Three Rivers, drive north on California Highway 198 for approximately 3.9 miles to Mineral King Road. Turn right (east), and follow the road for 10.1 miles to the Lookout Point entrance station. Continue east, losing and regaining pavement before passing Atwell Mill Campground. You lose and regain the

Cold Springs Nature Trail

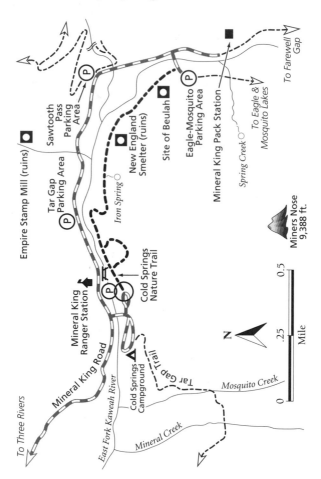

To Farewell Gap

To Eagle &
Mosquito Lakes

Sawtooth Pass
Parking Area

Eagle-Mosquito
Parking Area

Empire Stamp Mill (ruins)

New England
Smelter (ruins)

Site of Beulah

Mineral King Pack Station

Spring Creek

Tar Gap
Parking Area

Iron Spring

Miners Nose
9,388 ft.

Cold Springs
Nature Trail

Mineral King
Ranger Station

.5

.25   Mile

N

0

Mineral King Road

Cold Springs
Campground

Tar Gap Trail

Mosquito Creek

East Fork Kaweah River

To Three Rivers

Mineral Creek

pavement again before Cabin Cove and the Silver City Store and Resort at 20.5 miles. The road loses and regains pavement once more before reaching the Mineral King Ranger Station at 23.2 miles. Park at the picnic area on the south side of the road, across from the ranger station, or at the small turnout across from the Cold Springs Campground entrance.

Key points:
0.0 Trailhead.
0.8 Reach the smelter ruins.
1.0 Reach the site of Beulah.
1.8 Meet the nature loop.

The hike: The trail begins by passing through an open, grassy area, filled with meadow goldenrod, Bigelow's sneezeweed, and many other wildflowers in the summer. You come to the first interpretive sign as you enter cottonwoods and aspens. The interpretive signs identify the native plants and trees growing in the Mineral King Valley. When the trail forks, take the path to the left (east); the other path is part of your return trip. Pass the junction with the other portion of the interpretive trail and continue straight ahead, passing a couple of nice places to rest or eat lunch along the river.

The trail climbs briefly over a small rise, then dips to cross two small brooks on plank bridges in a hillside meadow. Enjoy the nice view down to the sparkling East Fork of the Kaweah River below as the path climbs a couple of switchbacks and enters a grove of firs. The trail then dips to cross a boggy hillside meadow watered by Iron Spring. Sierra gentians bloom profusely here in late summer. Ahead of you and across the valley is Black Wolf Falls, with Empire Mountain and Sawtooth Peak towering above.

The flat area of sagebrush that follows has views of Florence and Tulare Peaks to the south. At 0.8 mile, you will reach the site of the New England Smelter, just before a grove of aspen. Some foundation supports are all that is left of the smelter, which was used in the late 1800s.

Mineral Peak becomes visible to the right (south) of Sawtooth Peak prior to entering the aspen grove. The route winds through sagebrush mixed with flowers, and Rainbow Mountain joins Florence and Tulare Peaks and Farewell Gap in your view to the south. Proceed through a private residential area near tall fir trees. At 1 mile, arrive at the small sign marking the site of Beulah, a community that thrived during Mineral King's mining days. An avalanche set off by the San Francisco earthquake in 1906 leveled most of Beulah. Now private cabins occupy the town site.

The road ahead leads down to the Eagle-Mosquito parking area, passing through private cabins, each signed with family names and the year it was built. If you venture down to the parking area, stay on the road and respect the private property.

When you are ready to return, retrace your steps to the trail fork at 1.8 miles and turn left (south) to travel the other portion of the interpretive trail. You will arrive at the trailhead at 2 miles.

16
WHITE CHIEF CANYON

Highlights: This trek to a magnificent alpine bowl passes the ruins of a cabin, an expansive meadow, mine shafts, and marble caverns along the way.

Type of hike: Out-and-back.

Total distance: 8.2 miles.

Best months: July through September.

Elevation change: 2,150 feet.

Maps: USGS Mineral King; Sequoia National Park Mineral King; or TOPO! Sequoia Kings Canyon CD-ROM.

Special considerations: This trail is used by horseback riders. Please remember proper trail etiquette by stepping off the trail on the downhill side and waiting quietly until the horses have passed. Stay in plain view of the horses; they may think you are a wild animal and bolt if you are hidden behind a rock or tree.

Parking and trailhead facilities: The trailhead has a "Charge a Call" phone, but no rest rooms or water. The nearest rest rooms are located at the Sawtooth Pass parking area or across the road from the Mineral King Ranger Station. The trail begins at the south end of the parking area.

Finding the trailhead: From central Three Rivers, drive north on California Highway 198 for 3.9 miles to Mineral King Road. Turn right (east) and follow the road for 10.1 miles

White Chief Canyon

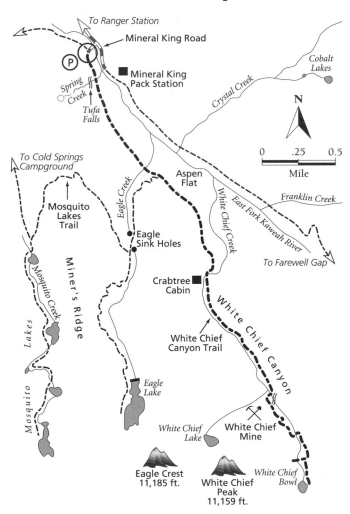

to the Lookout Point entrance station. Continue east, passing Atwell Mill Campground, then Cabin Cove and the Silver City Store and Resort at 20.5 miles. Reach the Mineral King Ranger Station at 23.2 miles. The parking area is 1.3 miles farther down the road, to the right and across a wooden bridge. Pass the Sawtooth Pass parking area and a junction with a dirt road leading to the pack station on the way.

Key points:
0.0 Trailhead.
0.3 Cross Spring Creek.
0.9 Ford the shallow waters of Eagle Creek.
1.0 Reach a trail junction.
2.0 Cross White Chief Creek.
2.9 Arrive at White Chief Mine.
4.1 Reach White Chief Bowl.

The hike: The trail begins with a slight ascent, passing the restored Honeymoon Cabin. Sagebrush and avalanche-thinned firs and junipers grow here, while delicate wildflowers add splashes of color. At 0.3 mile you cross Spring Creek on a wooden footbridge below Tufa Falls, which comes from a spring high above you on the canyon wall. The Farewell Gap Trail is visible across the canyon, along the east bank of the East Fork of the Kaweah River.

After the creek crossing, a horse trail from the pack station across the river joins your route. Look east for a view up the cascades of Crystal Creek, tumbling down to the right (south) of Mineral Peak. Tulare Peak is to the southeast; the silver ribbon to its left (north) is Franklin Creek. Look to the north to see Timber Gap and Empire Mountain high above the valley floor.

After stepping through the shallow waters of Eagle Creek at 0.9 mile, the climb steepens. At 1 mile the trail forks; continue straight (south) up the steep path. The route nears White Chief Creek, which is lined with blocks of metamorphic stone. Travel through jagged rock, and reach the usually dry crossing of the creek at 2 miles. Due to the porous nature of the marble in this area, White Chief Creek flows underground in some places. The meager ruins of Crabtree Cabin are to the right (west), just before the creek crossing.

The path follows the edge of White Chief Meadow, which is closed in by towering granite walls. It then climbs through forest, passing a primitive camping area on the right (west). When the trail leaves the trees, a pretty waterfall comes into view at the lower portion of the canyon. As you near the waterfall, look west across the canyon to the right of White Chief Peak; you can spot the creek trickling down from White Chief Lake. A footpath continues to the base of the falls. Your route is the dim track that splits off to the right (west), leading down to a rock-hop of White Chief Creek and the continuation of the trail.

At 2.9 miles, the route passes several shafts of the White Chief Mine as it switchbacks through marble and metamorphic rock. At the upper bench of the canyon, you pass sinkholes and marble caverns before another usually dry crossing of the creek. Do not attempt to enter any of the mine shafts or caverns; such exploring is very dangerous!

At the next junction. the right (west) fork leads to the ruins of a cavern-turned-homestead and to a large sinkhole. Take the left (south) fork to White Chief Bowl. After passing through overgrown willows you arrive at the canyon's end. Steep rock walls, verdant meadows, and a small tarn await you at 4.1 miles. Hummingbirds flit overhead, chattering as if you are there to challenge their food source, while Vandever Mountain towers above to the left (southeast) in dark and brooding colors. When you have enjoyed the alpine scene, return the way you came (8.2 miles).

17
FIRST MOSQUITO LAKE

Highlights: This hike makes a nice trip to a pretty lake, perfect for a picnic lunch with time to relax on the shore.

Type of hike: Out-and-back.

Total distance: 7.2 miles.

Best months: July through September.

Elevation change: 1,800 feet.

Maps: USGS Mineral King; Sequoia National Park Mineral King; or TOPO! Sequoia Kings Canyon CD-ROM.

Parking and trailhead facilities: The trailhead has a "Charge a Call" phone, but no rest rooms or water. The nearest rest rooms are located at the Sawtooth Pass parking area, or across the road from the Mineral King Ranger Station. The trail begins at the south end of the parking area.

Finding the trailhead: From central Three Rivers, drive north on California Highway 198 for 3.9 miles to Mineral King Road. Turn right (east) and follow the road for 10.1 miles to the Lookout Point entrance station. Continue east, losing and regaining pavement before passing Atwell Mill Campground. You lose and regain the pavement again before Cabin Cove and the Silver City Store and Resort at 20.5 miles. The road loses and regains pavement once more before reaching the Mineral King Ranger Station at 23.2 miles. The parking area is 1.3 miles farther down the

First Mosquito Lake

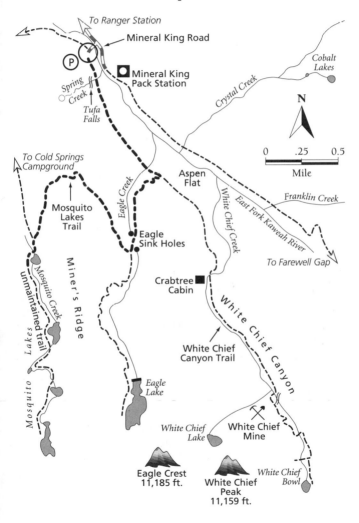

To Ranger Station

Mineral King Road

P

Spring Creek

Mineral King Pack Station

Cobalt Lakes

Crystal Creek

Tufa Falls

N

0   .25   0.5
Mile

To Cold Springs Campground

Aspen Flat

Franklin Creek

Mosquito Lakes Trail

Eagle Creek

White Chief Creek

East Fork Kaweah River

Eagle Sink Holes

To Farewell Gap

Miner's Ridge

Crabtree Cabin

White Chief Canyon

Mosquito Creek

unmaintained trail

White Chief Canyon Trail

Eagle Lake

Mosquito Lakes

White Chief Lake

White Chief Mine

White Chief Bowl

Eagle Crest
11,185 ft.

White Chief Peak
11,159 ft.

road, to the right and across a wooden bridge. You pass the Sawtooth Pass parking area and a junction with a dirt road leading to the pack station on the way.

Key points:
0.0 Trailhead.
0.3 Cross Spring Creek.
1.0 Reach the Eagle-Mosquito Trail junction.
2.0 Reach the Mosquito Lakes Trail junction.
3.6 Arrive at the first Mosquito Lake.

The hike: Begin by following the trail to White Chief Canyon (Hike 16). You cross Spring Creek on a wooden bridge at 0.3 mile, and reach a trail junction at 1 mile. Turn right (west). As you ascend steep switchbacks, the pack station appears diminutive far below. The route continues to climb, bringing you through a thick patch of woods to a steeply sloped meadow and more switchbacks.

Leveling off, the trail follows the dry canyon of Eagle Creek before arriving at the Eagle Sink Holes. Here Eagle Creek disappears into a large, deep crater and flows underground, leaving its former streambed dry. Another sinkhole can be found farther down the one-time watercourse. It is possible that Spring Creek, which you crossed earlier, receives its water from a subterranean stream originating in this area.

A few more switchbacks and you reach the Mosquito Lakes Trail junction at 2 miles. Turn right (northwest). The trail passes through a grassy meadow before winding up the slope. As you pass by the talus, watch for pikas, a tiny animal related to the rabbit. The views across Mineral King Valley to Sawtooth and Mineral Peaks in the east are breathtaking. Behind you and to the south is dark and craggy Vandever Mountain.

The path steadily ascends Miner's Ridge through a shady fir forest. Switchbacks up give way to short switch-backs down, and you descend through purple lupine to reach the first Mosquito Lake at 3.6 miles. Camping is not allowed at this lake but it makes a good place to take a lunch break.

When you have finished exploring the lake, retrace your steps over Miner's Ridge and return to the parking area at 7.2 miles.

Option: An unmaintained trail crosses the lake's outlet, passing a much steeper unmaintained route that leads down Mosquito Creek to Cold Springs Campground. You can easily take the unmaintained trail to the south side of the lake. Beyond, the path becomes more rugged and harder to follow.

18
LADYBUG CAMP

Highlights: This trip follows the first portion of the historic Hockett Trail, a trans-Sierra route built in the 1860s. The trail leads to secluded campsites along the South Fork of the Kaweah River.

Type of hike: Out-and-back.

Total distance: 3.8 miles.

Best months: Mid-March through May, October through mid-November.

Elevation change: 900 feet.

Maps: USGS Dennison Peak and Moses Mountain, or TOPO! Sequoia Kings Canyon CD-ROM.

Special considerations: Mountain lions frequent this area. You are advised not to hike solo.

Parking and trailhead facilities: Rest rooms are located in the South Fork Campground. Day use parking is west of the campground. Overnight parking is located farther down the road, east of the campground, at the trailhead. The trail begins at the east end of the overnight parking area.

Finding the trailhead: From central Three Rivers, follow South Fork Drive southeast, then east, to the Sequoia National Park boundary, where you lose the pavement. Continue on the dirt road to South Fork Campground, approximately 13 miles total.

Ladybug Camp

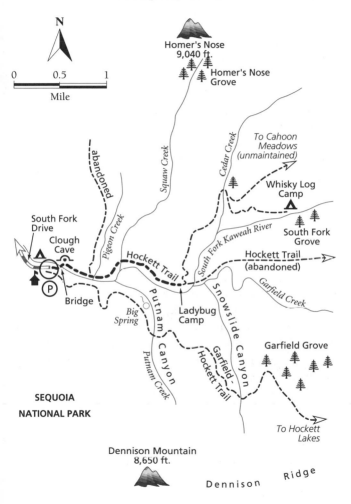

Key points:
0.0 Trailhead.
0.3 A side trail leads to Clough Cave.
0.5 Cross Pigeon Creek.
1.0 Cross the log over Squaw Creek.
1.9 Reach Ladybug Camp.

The hike: The trail sets off along the south bluff of the South Fork of the Kaweah, then crosses the river on a long wooden footbridge. On the other side, the trail climbs briefly. At 0.3 mile, a dim side trail to the left (north) leads to Clough Cave, home to a colony of endangered bats. The side trail rises uphill, becoming narrow and washed out just before the cave. Bars have been installed at the entrance due to the vandalism this cave has suffered.

The main route leads east along a rocky trail, through the shade of oaks and cedars. Watch out for the abundant poison oak. Side trails branch off toward the river, and a long-abandoned trail climbs to Salt Creek Ridge just before you reach the rarely flowing Pigeon Creek at 0.5 mile.

Continue east, traversing high above the river on rocky shelves. Look south across the canyon for a view of a waterfall on Putnam Creek. The trail curves into the Squaw Creek canyon and crosses the watercourse on a small log at 1 mile. The path then swings back to the southeast, with views across the South Fork to Dennison Ridge. Flat areas appear along the river below and you reach a signed junction above Ladybug Camp at 1.9 miles.

Follow a footpath down to Ladybug Camp, where you

can find wintering ladybugs on the underside of fallen leaves during the cooler months of the hiking season. Be careful not to harm them as you explore. When you have returned to the junction, follow the east-trending path to its demise at the river. The metal stakes that stick up through the granite mark the site of an old bridge; it collapsed in 1969 due to an exceptionally heavy snowpack.

On the other side of the river is the continuation of the historic Hockett Trail, which was constructed to transport supplies to the silver mines on the east side of the Sierra Nevada. It is now quite overgrown up to the point where it joins the Garfield-Hockett Trail, which also leads into the backcountry. Across the river, near the confluence of Garfield Creek, stands a solitary sequoia growing at one of the lowest elevations in the world. It is thought that, as a seedling, this tree was washed down the slope from the Garfield Grove in an 1876 landslide.

Return the way you came (3.8 miles).

Mitchell Peak

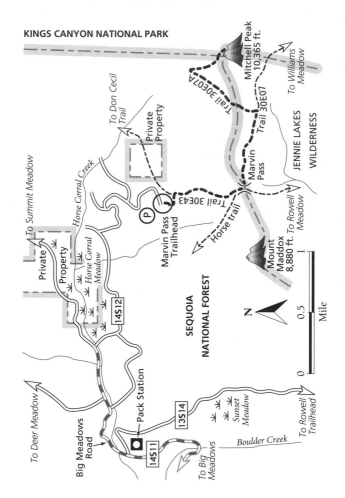

19
MITCHELL PEAK

Highlights: This trip takes you to a spectacular 360-degree vista on top of a windswept 10,365-foot peak.
Type of hike: Out-and-back.
Total distance: 6.4 miles.
Best months: Mid-June through October.
Elevation change: 1,995 feet.
Maps: USGS Muir Grove; USFS Monarch and Jennie Lakes Wilderness; or TOPO! Sequoia Kings Canyon CD-ROM.
Special considerations: During storms, there is a risk of being struck by lightning on the summit of Mitchell Peak. If you see dark clouds nearby, or observe hail, rain, thunder, or static electricity in the air, descend immediately.

Due to heavy use by horseback riders, the best times to hike this trail are early or late in the season. If you meet horses on the trail, remember it is proper trail etiquette to step off the trail on the downhill side and wait quietly until the horses have passed. Stay in plain view of the horses; they may think you are a wild animal and bolt if you are hidden behind a rock or tree.
Parking and trailhead facilities: There are no facilities at this trailhead except a small campsite at the north end of the parking area. The nearest rest rooms are at the Big Meadows Trailhead, 7.8 miles back down Forest Road 14S11. The trail begins at the south end of the parking area.

Finding the trailhead: Drive 9 miles south from Grant Grove on the Generals Highway to signed FR 14S11 to Big Meadows, just past the Big Baldy Trailhead. Turn left (northeast) and follow the road past the ranger station, Big Meadows Trailhead, and the campgrounds. The road narrows, crosses Big Meadows Creek, and passes a few spur roads before entering a deep canyon and crossing Boulder Creek at a large curve. Pass the road signed for the pack station, Sunset Meadow, and Rowell Meadow Trailhead, and cross Horse Corral Creek. At 18.3 miles, you will reach the second dirt road on the right, FR 14S12, signed for Marvin Pass Trailhead. Turn right (south) and follow the rough dirt road, passing several spur roads. It is easy to distinguish the main road until you reach the last unsigned spur road. It continues straight ahead (east), while you turn right (south) on FR 14S12, following the well-used road to its end at the trailhead parking area at 20.6 miles.

Key points:
0.0 Trailhead.
0.2 Pass a trail to private property.
1.0 Crest Marvin Pass.
1.7 Meet the Mitchell Peak Trail.
3.2 Reach the top of Mitchell Peak.

The hike: The Forest Service trail, FS 30E43, follows an abandoned logging road for just a few feet before abruptly turning south at a wooden trail sign. The dusty path climbs to cross a ridge, turns east, and passes through a level logged area where currants, manzanita, and snowbrush grow. Marvin Pass is the low wooded gap to the right (south). A trail that leads to private property is at 0.2 mile.

Turning south again, you rock-hop a small brook and skirt a meadow clipped short by grazing cattle. The trail ascends several switchbacks. You may notice a horse trail to your right, which comes up from one of the spur roads you passed on your drive to the trailhead. The trail crests timbered Marvin Pass at 1 mile and enters the Jennie Lakes Wilderness. This is a good place to rest and refuel.

The Marvin Pass Trail continues straight (south), downhill and on to Rowell Meadow. At the junction you turn left (east) and follow FS 30E07 between two large boulders toward Mitchell Peak. The route rises and dips, passing through shady forest and dry, sunny slopes dotted with lupine and red skyrockets. Meadows are visible here and there, below you on the right.

At 1.7 miles you reach the Mitchell Peak Trail, FS 30E07A, and turn left (northeast). The route climbs gradually at first. When it comes to a clearing you can see your destination—the rocky mountaintop on your right (east).

The path ascends more steeply and crosses the western ridge emanating from the peak. When the grade lessens, Horse Corral Meadow, where the last grizzly bear in California was shot in 1922, is visible through the trees, downhill to the left (northwest). As the slope becomes steep again, the trail turns to the south and winds up through a thinning forest of foxtail pines and an understory of lupines and phlox. When you reach the granite blocks, follow ducks (rock cairns) up through the talus that caps the peak. Some maneuvering through the blocks is necessary to attain the summit; go slowly and carefully.

Upon reaching a mostly level area you will see a pinnacle a few feet ahead of you at 3.2 miles. This is the high point of Mitchell Peak. If you do not wish to climb up to this roost you can still see the entire view by making your way to the west and east sides of the mountaintop. A concrete slab on the west side of the summit is all that is left of the Mitchell Peak Lookout, but it still provides a good spot to take in the views in all directions. A granite balcony on the east side of the pinnacle makes a great place to take in the views to the east and southeast.

To the northwest, the canyon of the Kings River, Spanish Mountain, and Obelisk are set against the backdrop of the John Muir Wilderness. On a clear day, you can see Dogtooth Peak in the Dinkey Lakes Wilderness. To the north are the Monarch Divide, Mount Goddard, and northern Kings Canyon National Park, and to the northeast is the headwaters country of the Kings River and Middle Palisade on the Sierra Crest. East of you is the Great Western Divide, with Sugarloaf and Sugarloaf Valley down below. The Kaweahs tower above all else to the southeast, and the Tablelands, Mount Silliman, Twin Peaks, and Kettle Peak fill the view to the south. Looking from the southwest to the west, you can see Poop Out Pass, Shell Mountain, Rowell Meadow, Mount Maddox, and even Buck Rock Lookout.

After you have delighted in this spectacular vista, return to the trailhead (6.4 miles).

20
WEAVER LAKE

Highlights: This enjoyable hike takes you to a striking lake, warm enough for swimming, at the base of Shell Mountain. The views along the way are superior.

Type of hike: Out-and-back.

Total distance: 6.4 miles.

Best months: June through October.

Elevation change: 1,475 feet.

Maps: USGS Muir Grove; USFS Monarch and Jennie Lakes Wilderness; or TOPO! Sequoia Kings Canyon CD-ROM.

Parking and trailhead facilities: A rest room is located at this trailhead and campsites are available at the south end, but there is no water. The old trail used to begin at the pay phone on Big Meadows Road, then climbed over the hill and passed through the campground to a sometimes wet crossing of Big Meadows Creek. The new trail starts at the northeast end of the parking area.

Finding the trailhead: Drive 9 miles south from Grant Grove on the Generals Highway to signed Forest Road 14S11 to Big Meadows, which is just beyond the Big Baldy Trailhead. Turn left (northeast) and follow the road past the ranger station, and former trailhead at the pay phone. The new Big Meadows Trailhead parking area is on the right (south) before the campground at 12.9 miles.

Weaver Lake

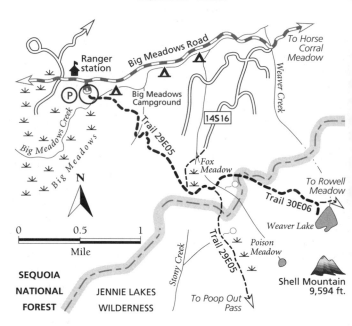

Key points:

0.0 Trailhead.

0.6 Cross an unnamed creek.

1.4 Pass an unmapped trail.

1.8 Reach the Jennie Lake Trail junction.

3.0 The Weaver Lake Trail forks.

3.2 Reach the shores of Weaver Lake.

The hike: The reconstructed portion of this trail, FS 29E05, leads downhill, through an area where several good campsites in Big Meadows Campground were unfortunately removed to accommodate it. Cross Big Meadows Creek on a new wooden footbridge to a four-way junction. A fisherman's trail heads south along the creek, and a footpath/cow trail leads uphill straight ahead, then over to Big Meadows. Your route is the well-worn path to the left (east), which soon comes to a trail register.

The trail travels uphill, around a granitic ridge, and follows an unnamed creek before crossing it at 0.6 mile. Climb to an open, sunny area where a side trail branches off to the left (northeast); it heads toward a barren ridgetop before rejoining the rocky main route. Your path reenters the forest and rises to cross a ridge. You soon have a view to the north of Spanish Mountain, Obelisk, and the Monarch Divide.

Another side trail, this time branching to the right (south), leads uphill and back to rejoin the main route. The trail descends to meet an unmapped pathway, leading up from FR 14S16, at beautiful Fox Meadow at 1.4 miles.

Wind around this patch of green surrounded by a dense woodland, then ascend through the thinning trees. At 1.8 miles, you reach the junction with the trail to Jennie Lake. Go left (northeast) onto FS 30E06 and immediately step across a creek tumbling down from a small, unnamed lake near the base of Shell Mountain.

Enter the Jennie Lakes Wilderness; the climb lessens a bit as the trail becomes rockier. You may see the top of

Shell Mountain peeking over the trees. The route spans a seasonal creek as well as the sometimes dry Weaver Creek, then arrives at trail signs and the short path to Weaver Lake on your right (southeast) at 3 miles.

A brief clamber through a rocky obstacle course deposits you on the shores of Weaver Lake at 3.2 miles, below the rugged face of Shell Mountain. There are campsites along the grassy shores and a large one just north of the lake, which is visible from the trail. After relishing the scenery, retrace your steps to the trailhead (6.4 miles).